The Wonders

of Speaking in Tongues

Key To Accessing The Supernatural

The Wonders of Speaking in Tongues

Mark Amoateng MD

1 Corinthians 14:2

Key To Accessing The Supernatural

The Wonders of Speaking in Tongues

All Rights Reserved

Copyright © 2015 by Mark Amoateng, MD

No part of this publication may be reproduced, stored in a retrieval system or transmitted in any way by any means, electronic, mechanical, photocopy, recording or otherwise, without the prior written permission of the author except as provided by USA copyright law.

All scriptures are taken from New King James Version of the Bible, unless otherwise quoted.

Author's Contact: stmarkone@yahoo.com

The opinions expressed by the author are not necessarily those of Rehoboth House.

Rehoboth House is committed to excellence in the publishing industry.

www.rehobothhouseonline com

EBook: 978-1-943281-28-2

Paperback: 978-0-9964267-1-8

Hardcover: 978-1-942526-42-1

Published in the United States of America by

Rehoboth House, Chicago.

Table of Contents

Dedication i

Introduction iii

CHAPTER 1
Your Connection To The Power Of God.................*1-24*
Praying In the Spirit Includes: 21
You Can Pray With Your Understanding 22

CHAPTER 2
When You Speak In Tongues Your Spirit Prays....*25-32*
Neuroscientific View of Speaking In Tongues 27

CHAPTER 3
You Speak Mysteries And Prays God's Will.........*33-52*
Speaking In Tongues Is A Great Tool of Intercession 34
Accessing The Will of God 35
Angels Released By Speaking In Tongues 37
Miraculous Delivery of a Baby 40
Missionary Delivered in Far Away Land 42
A Missionary's Encounter With a Buddhist 46
My Publisher's Experience 47
Speaking In Tongues is an Actual Language In Heaven 49
The Girl Who Saw Her Tongues 50

CHAPTER 4
Immune Deficiency Bolstered By Tongues............53-60
The Physical Benefit of Speaking In Tongues............................57
Immune Disorder Disgraced By Speaking In Tongues............59

Conclusion 61-62

Prayer Of Salvation...63-64

Other Book Written By The Same Author.....................65

References..66

Dedication

This book is dedicated to the precious Holy Spirit. There is none like Him. Precious Holy Spirit, if praise is like perfume, I lavish mine on you.

Introduction

"And it happened, while Apollos was at Corinth, that Paul, having passed through the upper regions, came to Ephesus. And finding some disciples he said to them, 'Did you receive the Holy Spirit when you believed?' So they said to him, 'We have not so much as heard whether there is a Holy Spirit.' And he said to them, 'Into what then were you baptized?' So they said, 'Into John's baptism.' Then Paul said, 'John indeed baptized with a baptism of repentance, saying to the people that they should believe on Him who would come after him, that is, on Christ Jesus.' When they heard this, they were baptized in the name of the Lord Jesus. And when Paul had laid hands on them, the

Introduction

Holy Spirit came upon them, and they spoke with tongues and prophesied" (Acts 19:1-7).

The purpose of this book is not to teach a doctrine, but to stir your heart into a greater dimension of spiritual manifestation. The baptism of the Holy Spirit with the manifestation of speaking in tongues is given to all believers. If you don't have the gift of speaking in tongues yet, I want to create in you the desire to speak in tongues. If you do have it, I want to stir you up to use it more often. But if you already have received the gift and speaks in tongues more often, I want to encourage you to maintain it and possibly increase your frequency of speaking in tongues.

The benefits of speaking in tongues are immense and the wonders are bewildering.

> *"The one who prays using a private "prayer language" certainly gets a lot out of it ..."*
> *1Cor 14.4-5 (The Message Bible).*

Speaking in tongues is one of the surest signs distinguishing the Old Testament believers from the New Testament believers.

> "And these signs will follow those who believe: In My name they will cast out demons; they will speak with new tongues; they will take up serpents; and if they drink anything deadly, it will by no means hurt them; they will lay hands on the sick, and they will recover." (Mark 16:17-18)

Speaking with new tongues according to Jesus' word in Mark 16 verse 17 is a sign that marks the New Testament Church. The Church was launched with the gift of speaking in tongues at the Upper Room in Acts of the Apostles.

> "When the Day of Pentecost had fully come, they were all with one accord in one place. And suddenly there came a sound from heaven, as of a rushing mighty wind, and it filled the whole house where they were sitting. Then there appeared to them divided tongues, as of fire, and one sat upon each of them.

Introduction

> And they were all filled with the Holy Spirit and began to speak with other tongues, as the Spirit gave them utterance." (Acts 2:1-4)

Speaking in tongues can bring great and awesome things that the human mind cannot comprehend. You can have as much of God as you desire manifesting through your life and one of the avenues is through the gift of speaking in tongues. Speaking in tongues has enormous benefits that can impact on your spirit, your soul and your body. It has benefits for all three levels of living and can synchronize your soul and body with your spirit.

Even as you read this book you can be speaking in tongues and reap immediate results. Speaking in tongue is like mingling yourself with fire. Anytime you mingle with fire the results are immediate. Let us embark on this adventure to discover the benefits and testimonies of the wonders of speaking in tongues.

CHAPTER 1

Your Connection To The Power Of God

"He who speaks in a tongue edifies himself, but he who prophesies edifies the church" (1 Cor 14:4-5).

"But you, beloved, build yourselves up [founded] on your most holy faith [make progress, rise like an edifice higher and higher], praying in the Holy Spirit" (Jude 20). **AMP**

God is very specific in His instructions and leaves no room for ambiguity. The scripture admonishes us to build up ourselves on our most holy faith and it shows us how. It suggests that you are a spiritual architectural structure to be built.

> *"For we are God's fellow workers; you are God's field, you are God's building" (1 Corinthians 3:9).*

We are God's building. As a believer, the Bible says you are a house.

> *"You also, as living stones, are being built up a spiritual house, a holy priesthood, to offer up spiritual sacrifices acceptable to God through Jesus Christ" (1 Peter 2: 5).*

He says we are being built up into a spiritual house. Scriptures always explain themselves. You might not find all the explanation of a concept in one single scripture. One principle of the Kingdom of God that is replete in the Bible is the building of precepts upon precepts. The revelation of the word of God is progressive.

> *"For precept must be upon precept, precept upon precept; line upon line, line upon line; here a little, and there a little"* (Isaiah 28:10).

The spiritual house that God is building is meant to contain God in His fullness and majesty. The whole of God's power, glory and essence is meant to dwell in, and more importantly manifest through that house which we are as a corporate body and you are as an individual believer. The scriptures say you are the temple of the Holy Spirit.

> *"Do you not know that you are the temple of God and that the Spirit of God dwells in you?"* (1 Corinthians 3:16).

God's power is meant to pass through you to bless your world. You are designed to be a conduit of His inestimable power. It is similar to how electric energy that is generated at a power generation plant far from your home, is transmitted through an electrical process into the comfort of your home to become a blessing to you. The cable that conveys the invisible energy into your home is what you see and identify with. In the same vein, you are the cable that transmits the power of God generated from Heaven to bless mankind. Your life, which is the house that God is building, is not intended to be ordinary but a befitting edifice. See the Amplified rendition of Jude 20.

> *"But you, beloved, build yourselves up [founded] on your most holy faith [make progress, rise like an edifice higher and higher], praying in the Holy Spirit."*

Your life has to be built into an edifice. An edifice is not an ordinary building. For a building to qualify as an edifice, it must be important, imposing and conspicuous in the midst of other buildings. Many times it is a towering sky scraper. God's plan is to make you an edifice, not a mud house. You are designed for significance and empowered by the Holy Spirit to exercise dominion over the devil and the circumstances of life. You are meant to tower above your peers in every venture of life.

The house is to be built on your most holy faith. The foundation for this house which you are, is your Most Holy Faith. It is to be established and grounded on the Most Holy Faith. In Col. 2:7 the scriptures say, **"You should be rooted and built up in Him, and established on <u>the Faith</u>"**. Here Paul is talking about a specific type of faith. He uses a definite article 'the' to qualify faith. Your most holy faith in Jude 20 is also known as "The Faith" in Col 2:7. That faith is the faith of Jesus Christ. It is that faith Paul talked about in Gal 2.20;

> **"I am crucified with Christ: nevertheless I live; yet not I, but Christ liveth in me: and the life which I now live in the flesh I live by**

***the faith of the Son of God**, who loved me,
and gave himself for me." KJV*

When you got born again you received the faith of Jesus Christ. This is the kind of faith that Jesus functioned with while on earth and worked diverse kinds of miracles. It is the glorious faith of the Son of God. This faith is your inheritance at salvation, which God gave to you. It is called <u>the measure of faith</u>.

> *"For I say, through the grace given unto me, to every man that is among you, not to think of himself more highly than he ought to think; but to think soberly, according as God hath dealt to every man <u>the measure of faith</u>." (Rom 12:3).*

It is the faith of Jesus and also the faith of God. It is the desire of our Father in heaven that His children operate by His kind of faith. So He admonishes us to have His faith to operate with. In Mark 11:22, The Douay – Rheims version of the Bible says have the faith of God. And the BBE says Have God's faith.

The faith of Jesus Christ is the most holy faith. Having faith in God is different from having the faith of God. You can have faith in anything. People have faith in trees, cars, certificates, degrees, strength and their bank accounts. What makes the believer different is that he possesses the God kind of faith. This faith is the operation, working or the exercising of God's power.

> *"Buried with Him in baptism, in which you also were raised with <u>Him through faith in the working of God</u>, who raised Him from the dead" (Col 2:12).*

This faith is a spiritual energy that can heal, deliver, and work miracles. It can overcome every difficulty of life and set you above any limits. With this faith, you can reign in every circumstance of life including your ministry, marriage, education, business, just name it. Amazingly, this is your foundation as a believer. You don't lack faith, you don't lack spiritual energy.

Now, two people can read the same portion of the scripture in a meeting or even sing the same song, but the degree of the power of the Holy Spirit manifesting through them could vary. Why is this so when they are all founded on the same holy faith of Jesus? The reason is simply because one has built himself more on <u>the Most Holy Faith</u> as instructed by Jude 20. Consequently, he is enabled to generate greater amount of spiritual energy than the other person (with a smaller edifice) who has not built himself up on his Most Holy Faith. What you are required to do is to rise like a majestic edifice upon that foundation of the faith of Jesus. When this happens in your life, great waves of divine power will course through your life (edifice) and the stream of God's power will take over every aspect of your life.

How do you rise up like an edifice? Jude tells us: 'Praying in the Holy Ghost'. When you speak in tongues more often, you will begin to rise up and break forth into manifestation of the power of God that you never could have imagined. Spiritual virtues are released in your life and through your life to bless others. Speaking in tongues has been one of the secrets of many great men of God who walked in the extreme dimension of God's power.

Kenneth E. Hagin of blessed memory, said that speaking in tongues became one of the key spiritual exercises he engaged in constantly. In one of his books, he said that one of his regular practices was to read the word of God and speak in tongues for about six hours before any preaching engagement. Evidently, notable miracles and healings are recorded to the glory of God through his ministry, including raising the dead back to life. He is often referred to as the father or granddaddy of the 'Word of Faith' movement.

John Graham Lake, one of the greatest men of God who ever lived, was called the forerunner of God's latter rain. He raised the dead, cast out devils with such boldness and audacity while he lived. During an unprecedented outbreak of a deadly plague in South Africa, he was among the few who could minister to the sick and the dying patients. At that time there was an apprehension amongst most physicians that the man of God could be infected with the viral disease. On the contrary, he proved the local physicians wrong after the virus was placed on his body through an experiment. It was discovered that the virus could not survive on his body due to the life of Holy Spirit living in him. This experiment was actually verified under a microscope showing that the virus died instantly when placed on his body. The law of the Spirit of Life in Christ Jesus was at work on his body. Those who witnessed the experiment stood in amazement of the outcome.

This is the caliber of the man I am talking about that demonstrated incredible power of the Holy Spirit in his time.

He once made a profound statement revealing the greatest secret of his walk with God and the power and depth of the revelation of the Word of God that he constantly experienced. He said, "I want to talk with the utmost frankness and say to you, that tongues have been the making of my ministry. It is that peculiar communication with God when He reveals to my soul the truth I utter to you day by day in the ministry. Many times, I climb out of bed, take my pencil and pad, and jot down the beautiful things of God, the wonderful things of God that He talks out in my spirit and reveals to my heart." Notice what he said, "Tongues have been the making of his ministry." Do you want and desire such tremendous manifestation of God's power? Then the pathway has been revealed to you in this book.

Apostle Paul wrote about half of the New Testament and God wrought special miracles and healings through him. He said; *"I speak in tongues more than you all"*. He is actually saying that he speaks in tongues more often than all of the brethren in that assembly.

> *"I thank my God I speak with tongues more than you all" (1Cor 14:18).*

When you speak in tongues your spirit becomes robust and expanded so that great waves of God's power can flow through you to every circumstance of your life. Bible says we are changed from glory to glory as we behold the Lord.

> *"But we all, with unveiled face, beholding as in a mirror the glory of the Lord, are being transformed into the same image from glory to glory, just as by the Spirit of the Lord"* (2 Cor 3:18).

If you have studied a little bit of physics, you know that an atom consists of electrons that orbit around a central nucleus and the orbits are called energy levels. There are higher and lower energy a levels. But each electron occupies a particular energy level. When you increase the energy of an electron, it moves from a lower energy level to a higher energy level. The same rule applies in the spiritual.

I believe that there are energy levels called 'the glory' in the spiritual dimension of God. The way you are changed from glory to glory is to increase your spiritual energy level. How do you do that? By constantly speaking in tongues you can be connected to the power station of God. As you get connected, the Holy Spirit infuses your being with God's spiritual energy that can catapult you from one level of glory to another. This experience elevates you from one level of faith to another level of faith that can cause a progressive increase of glory in every area of your life.

Beloved, there are higher heights in God available to you. And one of the surest and fastest ways of accessing them is by constantly speaking in tongues. In 1Cor. 14:4, anyone who speaks in tongues edifies himself. You embolden and encourage yourself in the Lord. When you increase the frequency of your speaking in tongues you build up yourself and begin to walk in uncommon boldness and absolute confidence. Evidently, timidity and fear begin to lose their hold on you. It enables you to take giant strides of faith, daring the unknown to accomplish all that God has revealed to you.

When you speak in tongues, you elevate yourself in the spirit. You charge up your spirit man for the manifestation of power. You set yourself ablaze as you speak in tongues.

Speaking in tongues is a key into the supernatural that unlocks the spiritual realm to you. It also allows you to operate in the gifts of the Holy Ghost. Paul tells Timothy to fan into flames, or rekindle or stir the gift of God in him. One of the ways of fanning into flames or rekindling the gift of God is through frequent speaking in tongues. You can accelerate your operation in the gifts of the Holy Ghost by speaking in tongues very often.

> **"Wherefore I put thee in remembrance that thou stir up the gift of God, which is in thee by the putting on of my hands."**
> **(2 Tim 1:6) KJV**

Do you want to see God's power in your life and ministry? Then endeavor to speak in tongues more often. You can speak in tongues in the car, on the bus, in the bathroom, possibly anywhere. You don't have to always shout in tongues. You can speak in tongues quietly without becoming a nuisance to others. When you have the opportunity of speaking audibly you can blast in tongues at the top of your voice. Speaking in tongues increases your capacity to receive divine mysteries and make you a conduit of God's power.

In Isaiah 54:1, God promises great abundance and increase.

> *"Sing, O barren, you who have not borne! Break forth into singing, and cry aloud, you who have not labored with child! For more are the children of the desolate than the children of the married woman," says the Lord"* (Isa 54:1).

But in verse 2, He shows them what to do to receive such abundance.

> *"Enlarge the place of your tent, and let them stretch out the curtains of your dwellings; Do not spare; Lengthen your cords"* (Isa 54:2).

Enlarge your tent. God has great things for you. He has awesome things for your marriage, ministry, and business but you must increase your capacity to receive. God has great vision and plans for you but till you increase your capacity to receive, you might only see a little portion of God's power in your life. God is like the ocean. How much you get of Him in your life depends on your capacity to receive, and one of the surest means of increasing your capacity is by speaking in tongues.

In 2 Kings 4, Elisha came to a woman who needed a miracle desperately from God. The issue was not whether God will give her a miracle. Rather, it was about her capacity to receive the miracle. Elisha told her to get vessels, in other words, woman expand your capacity to receive the deluge of miracles God is bringing in your life. The vessels represented the capacity of the woman. The oil flowed continuously to fill the entire capacity of the woman until she had no more room to receive. When her capacity was exhausted, the oil ceased. What if the woman had a billion vessels? The oil would have continued till they were all full. I am saying the same thing to you my dear friend. Increase your spiritual size. Increase your capacity to receive from God. How? By speaking in tongues and building up on your most holy faith. This spiritual exercise increases your spiritual capacity to receive all that God is bringing into your life.

What do you do when God is giving you a big dream and you are finding it difficult to see the vastness of His dream for your life? At such times, I encourage you spend quality time speaking in tongues, releasing mysteries through your inner man. If you remain focused and consistent, divine illumination will begin to flood your mind and suddenly you will tap into God's frequency to decode what He has been trying to communicate to you.

Before I progress further on this subject, I want to make a distinction here. There is a difference between **praying in the Spirit** (Jude 20) and then **praying with the spirit** (1 Cor14:14-

15). Praying in the Spirit includes all manner of prayers that are done through or by the inspiration of the Holy Spirit. Praying with the spirit talks about praying with your human spirit, and that is speaking in tongues. Paul refers to speaking in tongues as praying with the spirit.

> *"For if I pray in a tongue, my spirit prays, but my understanding is unfruitful" (1Cor 14:14-15).*

But when you are praying with the spirit you are certainly praying in the Holy Ghost. According to Ephesians 6:18, praying in the Spirit includes all manner of prayers and requests.

> *"<u>Praying always with all prayer and supplication in the Spirit</u>, being watchful to this end with all perseverance and supplication for all the saints — and for me,*

that utterance may be given to me, that I may open my mouth boldly to make known the mystery of the gospel, for which I am an ambassador in chains; that in it I may speak boldly, as I ought to speak" (Eph. 6:18-20).

Praying in the Spirit includes the following.

1. Praying with the spirit, (Speaking in tongues):

"For if I pray in a tongue, my spirit prays, but my understanding is unfruitful." (1 Cor. 14:14)

2. Groaning in the Spirit:

"Likewise the Spirit also helps in our weaknesses. For we do not know what we should pray for as we ought, but the Spirit Himself makes intercession for us with groanings which cannot be uttered." (Rom. 8:26)

3. You Can Pray With Your Understanding Under The Utterance Of The Spirit:

> *"What is the conclusion then? I will pray with the spirit, and I will also pray with the understanding. I will sing with the spirit, and I will also sing with the understanding." (1Cor. 14:15)*

But our attention in this book is on speaking in tongues, also known as praying with your spirit and it automatically qualifies for **praying in the Holy Spirit.**

In Romans12:11, Paul says never be lacking in zeal, keep your spiritual fervor. I like how The Message Bible renders it.

> *"Don't burn out; keep yourselves fueled and aflame. Be alert servants of the Master."*

Beloved, you don't have to burn out or lack in zeal and the fire of God as a believer. You don't have to run out of fuel. Paul said you have to keep yourself fueled and aflame. How do you do that? Speak in other tongues. Now you don't have an excuse to get colder by the day, because the means of staying on fire has been revealed to you. Hallelujah. When you speak in other tongues it is like you are at the gas station fueling yourself or filling your spiritual tank for your ride in life.

Your Connection To The Power Of God

CHAPTER 2

When You Speak In Tongues Your Spirit Prays

For if I pray in an unknown tongue, my spirit prayeth, but my understanding is unfruitful. (1 Cor.14.14) KJV

When you speak in tongues it is your spirit that is praying. Your mind is unfruitful and cannot understand what you are saying. However, you can pray with your spirit and you can also pray with your understanding. Speaking in tongues bypasses your human intelligence. It directly connects you to the spiritual realm where you can have access to mysteries. The Bible admonishes us not to lean on our own understanding. You can connect yourself with the understanding of God by speaking in tongues. I am not in any way advocating mental redundancy.

We are designed by God as free moral agents having the capacity to think and articulate information. I believe in thinking. In fact our thought process controls the direction of our lives.

> *"For as he thinks in his heart, so is he"*
> *(Prov. 23:7).*

But before you engage in thinking engage speaking in tongues and divine ideas will flow freely. When you speak in tongues you begin to reason with the Spirit of God and great wisdom and depth of revelations are released to you.

"But there is a spirit in man, and the breath of the Almighty gives him understanding" (Job 32:8).

It helps you to understand deeper things from the breath of God, which is the Holy Spirit. When you speak in tongues your spirit engages the Spirit of God and divine understanding is imparted to you.

Neuroscientific View of Speaking In Tongues

Scientific research has now discovered what the Bible revealed centuries ago that when you speak in tongues your spirit is doing the praying, but your mind is not engaged.

This is a summarized research of the measurement of regional cerebral blood flow during glossolalia (speaking in tongues):

The passionate, sometimes rhythmic, language like patter that pours forth from religious people who "speak in tongues" reflects a state of mental possession, many of them say. Now they have some neuroscience to back them up. Researchers at the University of Pennsylvania took brain images of five women while they spoke in tongues and found that their frontal lobes - the thinking, willful part of the brain through which people control what they do were relatively quiet, as were the language centers. The regions involved in maintaining self-consciousness were active. The women were not in blind trances, and it was unclear which region was driving the behavior.

The images, appearing in the current issue of the Journal Psychiatry Research: Neuroimaging, pinpoints the most active areas of the brain. The images are the first of their kind taken during this spoken religious practice, which has roots in the Old and New Testaments as well as in Pentecostal churches established in the early 1900s. The women in the study were healthy, active churchgoers.

"The amazing thing was how the images supported people's interpretation of what was happening," said Dr. Andrew B. Newberg, leader of the study team, which included Donna Morgan, Nancy Wintering and Mark Waldman. "The way they describe it, and what they believe, is that God is talking through them," he said. Dr. Newberg is also a co-author of "Why We Believe What We Believe."

In the study, the researchers used imaging techniques to track changes in the blood flow in each woman's brain in two different conditions; once as she sang a gospel song and again while speaking in tongues. By comparing the patterns created by these two emotional and devotional activities, the researchers could pinpoint blood-flow peaks and valleys unique to speaking in tongues. Ms. Morgan, a co-author of the study, was also a research subject. She is a born-again Christian who says she considers the ability to speak in tongues as a gift. "You're aware of your surroundings," she said. "You're not really out of control. But you have no control over what's happening. You're just flowing. You're in a realm of peace and comfort, and it's a fantastic feeling."

Contrary to what may be a common perception, studies suggest that people who speak in tongues rarely suffer from mental problems. A recent study of nearly 1,000 evangelical Christians in England found that those who engaged in the practice were more emotionally stable than those who did not. Researchers have identified at least two forms of the practice, one ecstatic and frenzied; the other subdued and nearly silent.

The new findings contrasted sharply with images taken of other spiritually inspired mental states like meditation, which is often a highly focused mental exercise, activating the frontal lobes.

Beloved the word of God is forever settled in heaven. Anytime you engage in speaking in tongues you have switched to the spiritual realm. The Bible tells us to walk in the spirit. And one of the surest ways you can be conscious of walking in the spirit is by speaking in tongues. 1Cor. 14:2, says…, *"howbeit in the spirit, he speaketh mysteries to God." KJV*

Anytime you engage in speaking in tongues, you are in the spirit. The scripture says; "howbeit **in the spirit**". Speaking in tongues connects you instantly to the spirit realm where you have the privilege to dialogue with God without an interposing barrier.

When You Speak In Tongues Your Spirit Prays

CHAPTER 3

You Speak Mysteries And Pray The Will Of God

"For he that speaketh in an unknown tongue speaketh not unto men, but unto God: for no man understandeth him; howbeit in the spirit he speaketh mysteries." (1 Cor 14:2) KJV

When you pray in tongues you don't speak to men. You have direct access to the throne of God anytime, any day and from any place. You don't have to go through any protocols to get to God. You're direct on the line speaking mysteries to your heavenly Father. You speak mysteries about your life and about others. The scriptures say we don't know what to pray for and how we ought to pray about certain things, but the Holy Spirit helps our human limitations. When you speak in tongues you release petitions and intercessions, which you ordinarily couldn't have known on your own.

Speaking In Tongues Is a Great Tool of Intercession

Now concerning the will of God, a lot of people are confused and do not know how to access it. You have to understand that the will of God is within the Kingdom of God. The kingdom of God is a spiritual kingdom. But Luke 17:21 says the kingdom of God is within you. It is like what Solomon said in Ecclesiastics 3.11, that God has set eternity in your heart. So the will of God you are seeking and looking for is not far from you. It is right within the kingdom in your spirit.

Accessing The Kingdom of God

How do you access it? One of the ways is by speaking in tongues. 1 Cor. 2:11a, says *"...Even so no one knows the things of God except the Spirit of God."* As you begin to speak in tongues the Holy Ghost begins to reveal the will of God in to your spirit.

> *"...We have received the Spirit which is of God, that we might know the things that has been freely given to us of God." (1 Cor 2:12)*

As you begin to engage in speaking in tongues frequently, you will be accessing the will of God for your life and know exactly what you have to do and the course to take in life. It sharpens your spiritual sensitivity.

I strongly believe that encoded in the depths of your spirit is the secret knowledge of the will of God for your life. The reason why you were born and the path to take in life are all hidden and preserved in God's will for you. They remain elusive to you till the day you uncover them. Only by the enlightenment and quickening of the spirit of truth within us can we come to a conscious knowledge of this facts embedded deep in us. Oh the blessedness of speaking in tongues.

Again speaking in tongues is a great tool of intercession. When a burden of God is laid on your heart and you're not sure what to pray for or how to pray about it, begin speaking in tongues.

> *"Likewise the Spirit also helpeth our infirmities: for we know not what we should pray for as we ought: but the Spirit itself maketh intercession for us with groanings which cannot be uttered." (Rom. 8:26) KJV*

The Holy Spirit can seize your spirit and let you groan in tongues to intercede for others. If you will yield to such burdens only eternity will reveal the testimonies that you will wrought by such moments of prayer. Testimonies of such operations abound. Let me now share a few of them with you.

Angels Released By Speaking In Tongues

In Chapter 1 of the book "War Beyond The Stars" By Joel and Jane French, the author shared a stunning testimony that I want to share with you. A Jewish Rabbi went to visit a pastor friend called Tom Woodward in Pasadena, USA. The Rabbi had been baptized in the Holy Spirit and was to share his testimony with a local Full Gospel Chapter. As they toured Tom's church in Pasadena, it was the time of the men's Morning Prayer Meeting. When they came to the prayer room, they passed quietly without disturbing the men who were praying. As they approached the door to leave the room, one of the men began praying loudly in his heavenly language. Tom moved on as he was accustomed to this kind of prayer. However, the Rabbi lingered at the door.

You Speak Mysteries And Pray the Will Of God

After a short while, Tom approached the Rabbi and told him that it was time to leave, reminding him of the speaking engagement at a ladies' luncheon. More importantly, they must first return to the hotel to get ready for the meeting. But the Rabbi still bewildered placed his finger across his lips for about ten minutes, while Tom waited impatiently. Surely the Rabbi had experienced such a thing before. As Tom approached him again, he noticed that the Rabbi's countenance had changed. He was actually looking like someone who had seen a ghost. His complexion was white and he was in complete awe of what he saw. "What's wrong?" Tom asked. "Shhhh, silence!" the Rabbi commanded.

For about thirty minutes the Rabbi stood in the doorway listening intently to the prayer of the man in the prayer room. After a while there was silence. "Who was that man praying? What languages does he know?" The Rabbi asked, demanding an answer from Tom. " Tom responded, "He is an uneducated man here in the church." He knows no languages other than English. I know him well. I will introduce you to him so that you can verify for yourself."

Then the Rabbi told Tom that he had just listened to the most beautiful and perfect Hebrew that he had ever heard spoken. And the Rabbi was an astute student of Hebrew. He said for about fifteen to twenty minutes the man had been speaking praises to God in the most beautiful psalms in blank verse. "But the most amazing thing then happened," the Rabbi continued. "Still speaking in perfect Hebrew, the man switched from the psalms and began calling angels by name and sending them on missions. Angels were called by their Hebrew names and were sent on specific missions to aid those who needed help. Some were sent to aid missionaries in trouble, the name and location of the missionary also being mentioned in the Hebrew language." The Rabbi was visibly shaken. Never had he even remotely dreamed that such a thing could be possible. And, of course, Tom Woodward required some time to regain his composure.

Awesome! Dear friend, you are not without help. With your heavenly language you have the whole host of heaven at your disposal. What will you do now? It's up to you to decide. Remember, faith without action is dead and we can only please God when we act in faith.

> *"But without faith it is impossible to please Him, for he who comes to God must believe that He is, and that He is a rewarder of those who diligently seek Him." (Hebrews 11:6)*

Miraculous Delivery of a Baby

In my own life I have seen several miracles and wonders wrought by speaking in tongues. Here is one of them. One morning I was on duty at the hospital taking care of patients. I suddenly began to feel a burden in my spirit to pray for a pregnant lady friend I had not seen for about four months. Immediately, I attempted to reach her on phone but she did not respond to my call after several attempts. The burden was consistently growing stronger in my heart as I was working. Then, I started praying in the spirit for about 20 minutes. After a while, the burden began to ease until I felt an inner peace.

Later in the evening I received a call from this lady. She explained how she had given birth to her baby earlier in the day. She further said during delivery when she got to the stage to push the baby out, suddenly there were complications such that she could no longer push. I believe that at that point hopelessness began to flood her mind as she watched the medical team frantically trying to comprehend what was responsible for the sudden complications. They did all they could to put the situation under control, but to no avail. She possibly watched the medical team staring at her helplessly. Then suddenly, the situation began to improve as she mustered strength again to push, to the amazement of everyone in the labor room. After a while, the baby came out safe and whole beyond what anyone present could explain. So I asked her what time was all these? When she told me, I was amazed because it was exactly within the time frame I was speaking in tongues praying for her while at the clinic.

Glory be to God. The wonders of speaking in tongues are unimaginable.

Missionary Delivered in Far Away Land

In another incident, a missionary on furlough told this true story while visiting his home church in Michigan. "While serving at a small field hospital in Africa, every two weeks I traveled by bicycle through the jungle to a nearby city for supplies. This was a journey of two days that required camping overnight at midway point. On one of those journeys, I arrived in the city where I planned to collect money from a bank, purchase medicine and supplies, and then begin my two-day journey back to the field hospital. Upon arrival in the city, I observed two men fighting, one of whom had been seriously injured. I treated him for his injuries and at the same time talked to him about the Lord Jesus Christ. I then traveled for two days and camped overnight and eventually arrived home safely.

Two weeks later I repeated my journey. As I arrived in the city, I was approached by the young man I had treated. He told me that he knew I had some money and medicines. He said, 'Some friends and I followed you into the jungle, knowing you would camp overnight. We planned to kill you and dispossess you of your money and drugs. But just as we were about to move into where you camped, we saw twenty six armed guards that you were surrounded by.' At this point I laughed and said no, I was certainly all alone in that jungle campsite where I do spend the night. The young man insisted and said, no sir, I was not the only person that saw the guards. My five friends also did, and we all counted them. It was because of those guards that we were afraid to attack you and left you alone.

At this point in the sermon, one of the men in the Michigan congregation jumped to his feet and interrupted the missionary and asked if he could tell him the exact day this happened. The missionary told the congregation the date and the man who had interrupted told him this story: "On the night of your incident in Africa, it was morning here and I was preparing to go and play golf. When I was about to putt, I felt the urge to pray for you. In fact, the urging of the Lord was so strong that I called some men in this church to meet with me here in the sanctuary to pray for you. Please all the men who met with me on that day should stand up?"

All the men who met together to pray that day stood up. The missionary wasn't concerned with whom they were. He was too busy counting how many men he saw. There were twenty six. The same number of angels the young man saw surrounding me that night.

This story is an incredible example of how the Spirit of the Lord moves in mysterious ways. If you ever feel such prodding, go along with it and give yourself to prayer. Beloved, engage God in prayer. The arms of prayer can reach anywhere and to anyone.

A Missionary's Encounter With a Buddhist

A lady missionary from the West was on a mission trip to Asia. One day when she was passing by a Buddish temple the Lord told her to go into the temple. She was stunned and asked the Lord why and what for? The Lord insisted that she should go in as instructed, then she will be told what next to do. After a while, she reluctantly entered the temple and saw a man praying passionately to Buddha. The Lord told her to start praying in tongues. As she prayed in tongues for a while, the man who was praying to Buddha ran to her and asked her to introduce him to the God she was referring to. She was surprised as the man began to interpret what she was praying in tongues. He said she was telling him in his language that since Buddha could not help you all these years you have been asking him to intervene in your matter, I know the God who can help you overcome the challenges that have plagued your life this long. At that point, she understood what was happening and led the man to Christ, right inside Buddha's domain and ministered deliverance to him. When we pray and speak in tongues we utter mysteries.

My Publisher's Experience

In 1993 his mother was diagnosed and treated for cancer. As it is common with cancer survivors, she was scheduled for a biweekly chemotherapy. He said one of the days he was supposed to take his mother to the hospital, there was no money for the medical bill. The night before the appointment he went to a weekly service at his local church. After a brief teaching on the power of praying in tongues, the pastor instructed everybody in the congregation to identify a particular need in their life as he led the entire congregation in an unbroken hour of praying in the Holy Ghost. At that point he remembered the medical appointment scheduled for the next day. So, he singled out that financial need and began praying in tongues till the end of the service. The next day a friend of his came to his house early in the morning. He had actually planned to come the previous night (This was the night the prayers were going on in his local church) but could not. "He said I just wanted to give you some money from a business deal I closed the previous day." He eventually gave him the exact amount needed for the chemotherapy. That was how God provided to meet that urgent need.

As you are reading this book, you might have an urgent need in your life, if you can dare to trust God and spend time praying in tongues, God can send help from the least expected source. The wonders of speaking in tongues can be precise and astonishing.

Beloved, we can go on and on and on with verifiable testimonies

Speaking In Tongues is an Actual Language in Heaven

> *"Though I speak with the tongues of men and of angels, and have not charity, I am become as sounding brass, or a tinkling cymbal." (1 Cor. 13:1 KJV)*

> *"If I could speak all the languages of earth and of angels, but didn't love others, I would only be a noisy gong or a clanging cymbal." (New Living Translation)*

> *"I may be able to speak the languages of human beings and even of angels, but if I have no love, my speech is no more than a noisy gong or a clanging bell." (Good News Translation)*

The Bible says there are the tongues of men and the tongues of angels. I believe there are languages in heaven. And when you engage in speaking in tongues you begin to communicate in your heavenly language. In the book of Daniel 5:5-28, there was a strange event that took place. A finger appeared and wrote words on the wall which the wise men of Belshazzar could not interpret. It took the spirit of God upon Daniel to interpret it. I believe it was a heavenly language.

The Girl Who Saw Her Tongues

This story of Peter Tan, a minister of the gospel, will give us a picture of this heavenly language. There was a seven year old girl who started having visions of Jesus. Jesus started speaking to her at that young age taking her on trips to heaven. One day this girl started praying in tongues. The mother was a bit disturbed so she asked her daughter if she understood what she was praying about in tongues. The girl said yes I do. So the mother was startled and said to her, beside speaking in tongues, you also understand what you're saying? So they got this man of God who has had several trips to heaven to talk with her so that they will verify the experiences of this young girl.

The mother asked her, how she knew what she is praying about in tongues. The girl had a diary where she had written her tongues. So she brought it to her mother and the mother was shocked. The mum said to her, not only do you understand your tongues, you can also see it? So to authenticate her claim, the mother asked her to write out what she was saying while speaking in tongues. And she said I will try and she began writing the sounds, the transliteration and the interpretations as well. The man of God who had come to validate her experience was shocked, because he recognized one shape of the letters this seven year old girl had written. He was shocked because he had seen this shape before on top of a building in heaven. The same meaning he had received in heaven was the same meaning the girl gave to the shape. Halleluiah!

The tongues God gives you is not gibberish or some unintelligible or meaningless utterances. It is an actual language which God and the Heavenly host appreciates and respond to. From now, any time you are engaged in speaking in tongues be conscious you are speaking an actual language.

CHAPTER 4

Immune Deficiency Bolstered By Tongues

"He who speaks in a [strange] tongue edifies and improves himself, ..." (1 Cor 14.4 AMP)

Speaking in tongues edifies – builds you up. The Bible did not qualify which part of your being that tongues speaking builds. Paul did not tell us specifically that it only improves your spirit, soul or body. Your whole self is improved by speaking in tongues. Your spiritual health is improved, your mental health is improved and your physical health is also improved.

> *Isaiah 28:11-12 says, "For with stammering lips and another tongue will he speak to this people. To whom he said, this is the rest wherewith ye may cause the weary to rest; and this is the refreshing: yet they would not hear" (KJV).*

You are refreshed by speaking in tongues. After a day's work, you can be refreshed by speaking in tongues.

Research has revealed that speaking in tongues improves your immune system. Hallelujah. Speaking in tongues is a means of walking in divine health. I believe the divine life of God in your spirit is supplied to your body when you speak in tongues.

> *"But if the Spirit of him that raised up Jesus from the dead dwell in you, he that raised up Christ from the dead shall also*

***quicken your mortal bodies by his Spirit that dwelleth in you"* (Rom 8:11) KJV.**

It keeps you fresh and young. I believe it releases some anti-aging properties into your body chemistry. Glory be to God. If only you will dedicate yourself to this blessed provision of God, you will be translated into walking in divine health. I also believe that it makes you mentally alert and sharp. The Holy Spirit can easily remind you of things. As you engage the Holy Ghost in speaking tongues, He improves your memory and mental dullness vanishes.

I believe that depression and the spirit of heaviness can be lifted by speaking in tongues. This is because speaking in tongues connects you directly to the presence of God. Because in 1Corinthians 14:2, when you speak in unknown tongue you are talking directly to

God. And in His presence there is fullness of joy and pleasures forevermore. The joy of the Lord flows to you and that Joy is your strength. **"…….for the joy of the LORD is your strength."** (Neh. 8:10). Physical and spiritual weaknesses vanish. Lethargy is dissolved. In times of grief when your heart is broken and you cannot lift up yourself, begin to speak in tongues and the joy of the Lord which is your strength will energize and lift up your countenance. Hallelujah!

Anxiety and worry I believe can be destroyed by speaking in tongues. If you have to face a panel or go for an interview and you are tensed and nervous, speak in tongues and the refreshing and calmness of God will begin to gradually engulf your soul. When you feel discouraged and tired, speak in tongues and your physical energy will be renewed.

The Physical Benefit of Speaking In Tongues

God has made provision for you and me to be whole, to be well and to have access to His healing power. There is a study that has been done by Dr. Carl Peterson, MD (the husband of author and evangelist Vickie Jamison Peterson). This Study revealed that there is a healing power that can be released from our own bodies for our own benefit. Dr. Carl Peterson, MD worked on this Study at Oral Robert University (ORU) in Tulsa, Oklahoma a few years ago. Being a brain specialist, he was doing research on what the relationship was between the brain and praying or speaking in tongues. Some amazing things were discovered.

Through research and testing he found out that as we pray in the Spirit, or worship in the Spirit, (our heavenly language) there is activity that begins to take place in our brain. As we engage in our heavenly language the brain releases two chemical secretions that are directed into our immune systems giving a 35% to 40% boost to the immune system. This promotes healing within our bodies. Amazingly, this secretion is triggered from a part of the brain that has no other apparent activity or function in humans and is only activated by our Spirit led prayer and worship.

Before the fall of man, God in His perfect creation provided total healing for mankind. As Adam walked and communicated with the Father in the Garden, this close and intimate fellowship and communication caused divine health to flow in his body. This is just something for us to think about. God is the restorer of all things. As we exercise our life in the "Spirit" by speaking in our heavenly language that He has put in us, we are touching and drawing on the supernatural power of God, simultaneously letting Him restore part of what was lost at the fall.

Science has now proven the process and you can turn this healing process on by your relationship with our heavenly Father. This is just one more reason to be filled with the Holy Spirit and commune with the Father in your "Heavenly Language." According to the Holy Spirit, speaking through the apostle Paul: *"He who speaks in a tongue edifies himself"* (1 Corinthians 14:4). We have always thought of the edification as only being spiritual edification, which is great and is always needed, but Christian psychiatrist Carl R. Peterson, M.D. also describes physical edification. Isn't God amazing?

An Immune Disorder Disgraced By Speaking In Tongues

In my own experience, I have found the healing of immune disorder by speaking in tongues. Let me share this testimony with you. I was called to pray for a young lady who had an immune disorder in Houston Texas, USA. The condition was such that she would have very high temperature at night. When I got there, I asked if she was born again. She said yes. Then I asked if she speaks in tongues, she said no. I went on and taught her on the blessedness of speaking in tongues and how it can impact her health, especially her immune system. I laid my hands on her to receive the baptism of the Holy Spirit. Immediately she started speaking in tongues and spoke for the next fifteen minutes. She went to bed that night and through the glory and power of God she slept soundly like a baby. Her temperature was normal all through that night. Imagine, just fifteen minutes of speaking in tongues bolstered her immune system. She is now perfectly whole and well. Hallelujah!

Conclusion

Beloved, God's purpose is for you to experience all round rest in your life. He has provided you with the means through the avenue of speaking in tongues. As you get committed to speaking in tongues more frequently, times of refreshing will manifest from the presence of the Lord to your marriage, ministry, finances and every other area of your life, even academically. You will walk above the realm of diseases, your soul will be restored and your spirit man will be renewed. You will exchange your

Conclusion

natural plans for divine plans and a stream of God's power will flow through your life. But friend, you cannot enjoy this blessed benefits and experience this awesome wonders of speaking in tongues unless you are born again and make Jesus the Lord of your life.

Prayer Of Salvation

My dearest friend, to receive Jesus into your life and have the born again experience pray this prayer:

Dear Lord God, I come to you in the name of Jesus Christ. Your word says '....whosoever shall call on the name of the Lord shall be saved" (Acts 2:21). I declare that Jesus is the Lord of my life. I believe with all of my heart that He died on the Cross and was raised again to life on the third day. I receive the Life of God in my spirit now. I pray in Jesus' name. Amen.

If you prayed this prayer sincerely from your heart, you are now born again. You are a child of God and a royal citizen of heaven. All the gifts of God is now your inheritance. Now, begin to desire the baptism of the Holy Spirit and ask God to fill you with His Spirit. He will. Ask in faith knowing that you will receive because the scriptures says in Luke 11:11-13, **"...that your heavenly father will give the Holy Spirit to them that ask Him."**

God bless you richly in your new walk with Him.

Other Book Written By The Same Author

Reading this book *"The Wonders of Speaking in Tongues"* may have impacted your life in various ways. You have the privilege to read the other book written by the same author.

The subject of how to receive from God has been one of the most daunting challenges among most believers the world over. In this book, *"How to Receive From God: The Mechanism"* the author has simplified the biblical requirements of how to receive what God has freely given to us. *"As His divine power has given to us all things that pertain to life and godliness, through the knowledge of Him who called us by glory and virtue" (2 Peter 1:3).* As you read, I encourage you to approach the subject with faith in your heart.

References

This book would not have been completed without the sources quoted in it to accentuate the message and authenticating it through scientific proofs.

I give credit to the New Leaf Press Inc., Publishers of "War beyond the Stars" By Joel and Jane French and the life experiences of men of God like, John G. Lake, Kenneth E. Hagin of blessed memory and Peter Tan. I applaud the following Researchers at the University of Pennsylvania for their hunger to know the truth by scientifically authenticating the eternal and infallible word of God, Dr. Andrew B. Newberg, Donna Morgan, Nancy Wintering and Mark Waldman, and also Dr. Carl Peterson, a brain specialist at Oral Robert University (ORU) in Tulsa, Oklahoma who did a research on what the relationship is between the brain and praying or speaking in tongues.

www.ingramcontent.com/pod-product-compliance
Lightning Source LLC
Chambersburg PA
CBHW051956290426
44110CB00015B/2273